Bearded
Dragons

by Jody Jensen Shaffer

Content Consultant
Philip Bergmann
Department of Biology
Clark University

Core Library

An Imprint of Abdo Publishing
www.abdopublishing.com

www.abdopublishing.com

Published by Abdo Publishing, a division of ABDO, PO Box 398166,
Minneapolis, Minnesota 55439. Copyright © 2015 by Abdo Consulting
Group, Inc. International copyrights reserved in all countries. No part of
this book may be reproduced in any form without written permission from
the publisher. Core Library™ is a trademark and logo of Abdo Publishing.

Printed in the United States of America, North Mankato, Minnesota
032014
092014

THIS BOOK CONTAINS
RECYCLED MATERIALS

Cover Photo: Ashley Whitworth/Shutterstock Images
Interior Photos: Ashley Whitworth/Shutterstock Images, 1; Brooke
Whatnall/Shutterstock Images, 4; Maynard Case/Shutterstock Images, 6;
Eric Isselee/Shutterstock Images, 7; Reinhold Leitner/Shutterstock Images,
9; Shutterstock Images, 12, 39; Animals Animals/SuperStock, 15, 16;
S.C.Hpet/Alamy, 18; iStockphoto, 20, 28; Juniors Bildarchiv/Glow Images,
23; Cre8tive Images/Shutterstock Images, 26, 45; Red Line Editorial, 31;
iStockphoto/Thinkstock, 33, 43; Karl Johaentges/LOOK-foto/Glow Images,
34; Steimer, C./Arco Images/Glow Images, 37; Janelle Lugge/Shutterstock
Images, 40

Editor: Mirella Miller
Series Designer: Becky Daum

Library of Congress Control Number: 2014902276

Cataloging-in-Publication Data
Shaffer, Jody Jensen.
 Bearded dragons / Jody Jensen Shaffer.
   p. cm. -- (Amazing reptiles)
Includes bibliographical references and index.
ISBN 978-1-62403-369-8
1. Bearded dragons (Reptiles)--Juvenile literature.   I. Title.
597.95/5--dc23

                                                         2014902276

CONTENTS

Bearded Dragon Basics

It's dusk in the Australian Outback. A bearded dragon descends from its perch. It has been another long day of hunting and protecting its territory. The dragon needs to find shelter from predators and from the cool air.

On the ground, the dragon sees movement. A dingo! There is no time to run. The dragon faces the dingo. The dragon flattens its body so it looks bigger.

A bearded dragon uses its environment and special features to protect itself.

A bearded dragon's spiny throat and beard help scare predators away.

The dragon hisses and shows its teeth and mouth. The dingo does not move. The dragon puffs out its throat and extends its spiny, black beard. The spines on its head and body quiver. The young dingo jumps back and runs away. There are easier ways for the dingo to get dinner.

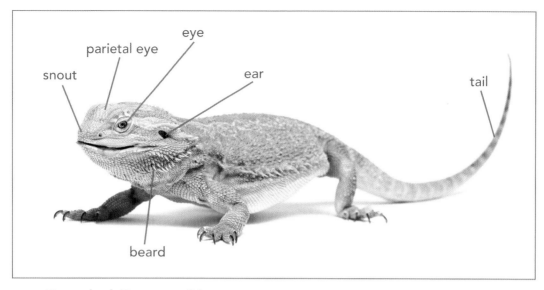

Bearded Dragon Diagram

Chapter One discusses many bearded dragon body parts. This diagram shows some of the physical characteristics of a bearded dragon. How might some of these parts help a bearded dragon look out for predators or detect prey?

For now the bearded dragon is safe. Next time it might not be so lucky. A more experienced predator may have known that bearded dragons are not as scary as they seem. The dragon runs to a rocky area to hide. It is safe for one more night.

Bearded Beauties

Bearded dragons are medium-sized lizards found naturally only in Australia. There are eight species of

The Third Eye

Bearded dragons have a third eye on the top of their head. It is called the parietal eye. This third eye is covered with a layer of skin and cannot actually see images. But it senses light and darkness. The third eye also helps bearded dragons control their body temperature.

bearded dragons. One of the most well known is the central bearded dragon.

Bearded dragons are named for the pouch under their throat. This pouch is called a beard. Dragons can puff out their beards and cause them to turn black. They do this to scare predators. Scientists are still studying how dragons are able to do this.

A dragon's throat is not the only remarkable part of its appearance. A dragon has thick, bumpy skin. Spines line the sides of its triangular head and body. These spines look sharp, but they are actually soft. The spines look scary to predators. Bearded dragons have strong tails that are as long as their head and body combined.

Bearded dragons come in a variety of colors, including orange.

Bearded dragons have thick legs and wide bodies. Their toes and claws are perfect for climbing. Male dragons have broader heads and more developed beards than females.

Bearded dragons are usually a combination of many colors. These include green, tan, yellow, and red. The color of their skin can turn lighter or darker based on the region and the soil. Their coloring also depends on their age. Male dragons are slightly more colorful than females.

Male bearded dragons grow to between 13 and 24 inches (33 and 61 cm) long. Females are a few inches shorter with smaller heads. Bearded dragons weigh between 10 and 18 ounces (283 and 510 g).

Sight is a bearded dragon's most important sense. It relies on sight to see its prey move. Some scientists believe bearded dragons can see in color. These lizards use other senses to experience the

Tasting the Air

Bearded dragons have an organ in the roof of their mouth that helps them smell. It is called the Jacobson's organ. As bearded dragons flick their tongues into the air, they pick up tiny, moist particles. Then they touch their tongues to their Jacobson's organ. It analyzes the substances found in the air.

world around them too. They have ear holes on the sides of their head. And they use their sticky tongues to smell the air.

Bearded dragons make a low hiss when confronted. This is the only noise they make. They communicate with one another mostly through movements and by changing their beard colors. They bob their heads, wave their legs, and lighten or darken the color of their skin.

EXPLORE ONLINE

The focus of Chapter One is the bearded dragon's appearance. The website below focuses on the appearance of central bearded dragons. As you know, every source is different. How is the information on the website different from the information in this chapter? What details are the same? How do the two sources present facts differently? What can you learn from this website?

Central Bearded Dragon

www.mycorelibrary.com/bearded-dragons

The Life of a Dragon

Mating season begins in the spring for bearded dragons. Because Australia is in the Southern Hemisphere, spring begins in September. The male begins the courtship ritual. He approaches a female and circles her. He waves one front leg and bobs his head. He changes his skin color and extends his beard. He may turn his beard black too.

As air temperatures rise in Australia, bearded dragons look for mates.

Bearded Dragons with Bite

Researchers at Melbourne University in Australia made an amazing discovery in 2005. They found out that bearded dragons have venom glands. These glands produce mild venom. The venom contains toxins previously found only in rattlesnakes. This venom can kill small prey but is usually not harmful to humans. Bearded dragons do not have fangs. They release their venom in their saliva.

If a female wants to mate, she waves one of her front legs and bobs her head.

Preparing for Dragon Babies

A female bearded dragon may carry between 14 and 26 eggs. Before she lays them, she basks in the sun more than usual. She also digs test holes to find the right spot to lay her eggs.

Two to three weeks after mating, the female uses her front claws to dig the final nest. She turns around and backs into it. Only her nose shows above ground. The female lays her eggs and crawls out of the nest. She loosely covers it with dirt. She may return to the nest for a few hours, but eventually she leaves it for good. Female bearded

Females lay their eggs in a sheltered environment that will help the hatchlings grow.

dragons lay several nests per year. That is more than 100 eggs each year!

Eggs and Hatchlings

Bearded dragon eggs are white and soft. The soil around them keeps them moist. The eggs incubate

Hatchlings must take care of themselves when they hatch from their eggs.

quickly when temperatures are warm. Hatchlings usually emerge after 78 to 85 days. They may weigh less than 1 ounce (28 g). Hatchlings are typically 1.5 to 4 inches (3.8 cm to 10 cm) long. Some have orange stripes near their eyes. These stripes fade over time.

Length	Age
3–4 inches (8–10 cm)	0–1 month
5–9 inches (13–23 cm)	2 months
8–11 inches (20–28 cm)	3 months
9–12 inches (23–30 cm)	4 months
11–20 inches (28–51 cm)	5–8 months
16–22 inches (41–56 cm)	12 months

Bearded Dragons' Age
It is easy to identify a bearded dragon's age based on its length. Use this chart as a guide.

Home Alone

Bearded dragons are alone from the time they hatch. Their parents do not protect the nest or the hatchlings from predators. Hatchlings are good at looking out for themselves. They are good hunters. They eat many kinds of insects. Hatchlings grow quickly if food is available.

Young bearded dragons spend their days alone. They search for food and bask in the sun. They protect themselves from predators by running away.

A bearded dragon molts its skin as the reptile grows larger and older.

Young bearded dragons reproduce when they are between one and two years old. The typical life span of a bearded dragon in the wild is four to ten years.

As bearded dragons grow, they shed their skin. This is called molting. Their skin molts in pieces or flakes. The outside temperature and availability of food determine how frequently bearded dragons molt.

When outside temperatures get cooler, bearded dragons enter brumation. Brumation is a kind of hibernation in which an animal's body temperature falls and its appetite decreases. During brumation, bearded dragons seek shelter under a rock or in a hollow log. They may not eat for two to three months. When outside temperatures rise above 54°F (12°C), bearded dragons eat and become active again.

FURTHER EVIDENCE

Chapter Two covers the bearded dragon's life cycle. What is one of the main points of the chapter? What key evidence supports this point? Check out the website below. Find a quote that relates to this chapter. Does this quote support the author's main point? Does it make a new point? Write a few sentences explaining how the quote relates to the chapter.

Inland Bearded Dragon
www.mycorelibrary.com/bearded-dragons

CHAPTER THREE

Dragon Tales

Bearded dragons' communication starts with their beards. They hiss at predators when they are threatened. But they communicate with other dragons by using their bodies.

Both males and females can expand the spiny pouch on their throats. They do this when they are threatened or excited. A bone-like rod on each side of their head moves out and pushes the skin. This makes

A bearded dragon uses its beard to communicate with other dragons and to scare away predators.

bearded dragons look bigger to predators. Males also extend their beards when courting females. Bearded dragons can make their beards turn black. This is a sign of dominance and excitement. It happens more often in males. The beard also darkens with age.

Another way bearded dragons communicate is by bobbing their heads up and down. An older male shows dominance over a younger male by bobbing his head quickly. He lets a female know he wants to mate with her the same way. A female may bob her head slowly to show she likes a male.

Leg waving is another way these lizards communicate. A dragon stands on three legs and

Move Over, Iguana

Although central bearded dragons are found naturally only in Australia, they can be found in pet stores worldwide. Bearded dragons are becoming increasingly popular as pets. Among reptile pets, bearded dragons are now more popular than iguanas in the United States.

Leg waving can be a sign of submission or friendliness.

waves its fourth front leg in a slow circle. Females show leg-waving behavior throughout their lives. Males eventually stop.

The Search for Food

Bearded dragons spend a lot of time looking for food. They are omnivores and are not picky eaters. They eat animals and plants.

Young bearded dragons eat small insects such as crickets. As they grow, they eat spiders, ants, beetles, small rodents, leaves, berries, fruit, and flowers. Adults also eat small lizards, including younger dragons.

Bearded dragons snatch insects from plants and flowers. Their teeth and strong jaws hold the food. They quickly kill or break apart the animal or plant before swallowing it.

Protecting Their Territories

Wild bearded dragons live alone. They do not form social groups with other dragons. Males are territorial and stake out large areas for themselves. If a similarly sized male enters the territory, the two may fight.

Before the males fight, the territory owner bobs his head as a warning. If the other male also bobs his head, it means he will not back down. Then both dragons flatten their bodies, hiss, and show their mouths. If these signals do not work, they circle and bite one another on the neck spines and tails. The winner pins the loser to the ground. The loser then runs away.

Females and young males occupy smaller ranges within a male's territory. When they encounter the male, they begin submission gestures, such as leg waving, to try to avoid a fight.

Protection from Predators

Bearded dragons must protect themselves from predators. They are vulnerable to birds of prey, such as eagles and hawks. Snakes, foxes, and feral cats are also predators.

When bearded dragons first see a predator, they try to blend into their environment. They may make their skin lighter or darker to match the soil on which they are standing. If that does not work, they run. If the

Now You See It, Now You Don't

Unlike some lizards that drop their tails when escaping from predators, bearded dragons don't. Their tails are still important, however. They use them for balance and to store extra fat. Their bodies use this fat when food is scarce.

A bearded dragon will try running away before scaring off a predator.

predator is too close for the dragon to get away, the dragon tries to intimidate it.

Bearded dragons also flatten their bodies to communicate to predators. They do this to appear bigger to predators. They are showing they are tougher than the predator.

The dragon opens its mouth, inflates its beard, and turns its beard black. The bearded dragon may also darken its entire body. It may hiss and make small jumps at the predator.

Chris Mattison is a wildlife photographer who is an expert on reptiles and amphibians. For years, he has studied bearded dragons' ability to live in very hot climates. In this passage, he explains the several ways dragons cope with extreme temperatures:

> *Small variations in posture and the angling of their body either towards or away from the sun enable them to raise or lower their body temperature as required. Raising the body away from the hot substrate and standing vertically at midday (stilting) is also a very effective thermoregulatory strategy, as is climbing up on twigs and branches during the hottest part of the day.*

*Source: Firefly Encyclopedia of Reptiles and Amphibians. Ed. Chris Mattison.
Richmond Hill, Ontario: Firefly, 2008. Print. 148.*

What's the Big Idea?

Take a close look at this passage. What is Mattison's main idea? What evidence does he use to support the points he makes? Come up with a few sentences showing how this passage uses two or three pieces of evidence to support the main point.

CHAPTER FOUR

A Dragon's Home

Bearded dragons can be found in a wide variety of habitats in Australia. These include subtropical deserts, dry forests, woodlands, and scrublands.

The deserts of central Australia are hot and sandy, with little rain and few plants. They are harsh environments. Temperatures can rise to more

Wild bearded dragons are found in many areas across Australia.

than 122°F (50°C). These deserts are very dry. They receive less than ten inches (25 cm) of rain per year.

Bearded dragons also live in dry forests and woodlands. Dry forests contain plants with short, spiky leaves. Bearded dragons are also found in scrublands with bushes that grow between 6 and 30 feet (2 and 9 m) tall.

Thriving in the Desert

Bearded dragons are perfectly suited to the hot, dry conditions where they live. They have developed several adaptations that allow them to thrive in these places.

One is the ability to make their skin lighter or darker. Blending in with the soil helps dragons avoid detection by predators. This is particularly important

Drinking Water

Bearded dragons can be made up of 70 percent water. But they live in dry areas without much rainfall or standing water. Bearded dragons get some of the water they need from plants. They also get water from some of the insects they eat.

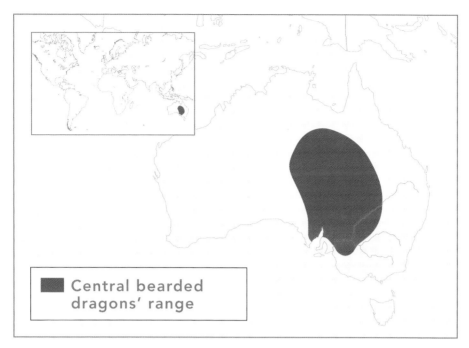

Central Bearded Dragons' Range
Look at the range map of the different places the central bearded dragon calls home. Why are bearded dragons well suited for these habitats? Write a short paragraph describing a central bearded dragon's habitat.

since there are few hiding places in their natural environments.

Some Like It Hot

Like all reptiles, bearded dragons are cold-blooded. They cannot make their own heat, so they get heat from the environment around them. To do this, bearded dragons bask in the sun.

Because bearded dragons are good climbers, they often bask on fence posts, tree limbs, or high rocks. Dominant males perch on the highest branches and basking areas.

Bearded dragons need to keep a body temperature of 95°F (35°C) to stay healthy. Dragons in the wild have body temperatures that change frequently throughout the day. There is plenty of sun for warmth in central Australia. Some areas within the bearded dragon's range have sunny days nearly 75 percent of the year.

Too Hot to Handle

When outside temperatures cause a dragon's body temperature to rise above 95°F (35°C), it takes steps

In order to warm their body temperature, bearded dragons climb on high objects to bask in the sun.

to cool down. Bearded dragons' skin turns light-colored. This prevents them from getting too hot. Light colors reflect heat. When temperatures drop, dragons darken their skin. Dark colors absorb heat.

Dragons have more ways of controlling their body temperatures too. They open their mouths to let out heat. They perch in trees to catch cool breezes. And they lift their feet off the hot ground one at a time.

CHAPTER FIVE

Natural and Man-Made Threats

Bearded dragons are not endangered. But that does not mean they do not face any threats. There are many natural threats to bearded dragons. Predators include birds, monitor lizards, and pythons. Dingoes, foxes, and feral cats also prey upon bearded dragons.

Man-made threats are forcing bearded dragons out of their habitats.

Sneaking In

Bearded dragons also experience man-made threats. One is smuggling. Between 1974 and 1990, people smuggled bearded dragons out of Australia. This is illegal. The dragons were taken to the United States, Europe, and Asia where they were bred. You can now legally purchase a captive-bred bearded dragon in many parts of the world.

On the Road Again

When the sun begins to set, bearded dragons bask on surfaces that have been warmed by the sun. These include roads. Many bearded dragons are killed this way. When driving through the Outback, it is important to be aware of wildlife. If you see a bearded dragon on the road, slow down. It may not move as quickly as you think.

Habitat Loss

Habitat loss is another man-made threat to bearded dragons. In Queensland and New South Wales, farmers clear land for agriculture. When land is cleared, trees, bushes, and shrubs are lost. Bearded

As land is cleared in Australia, it ruins the bearded dragons' habitat.

dragons have fewer places to hide and bask. They also have fewer plants to eat.

Feral Animals

Feral animals are another threat to bearded dragons. Some feral animals are pets that ran away from their owners. They survive, breed, and learn to live in the wild. Feral pigs, cats, and foxes prey on bearded dragons.

Problem with Feral Animals

Feral animals are a problem in Australia. They reproduce quickly and have few natural predators. Feral animals compete with native animals, like bearded dragons, for food and shelter. They destroy habitats and spread diseases. Plants help anchor soil and reduce erosion. Some feral animals eat young plants, which contributes to erosion. Erosion occurs when soil is swept away by wind or water. This leaves less growing space for the food bearded dragons eat.

Tourists

Humans who use areas where bearded dragons live are another threat to these animals. Australia's tourists and locals drive through, camp in, and sometimes destroy bearded dragon habitats.

Brighter Days Ahead

Despite these threats to bearded dragons, they are not endangered in Australia. Australians care deeply about protecting

Along with farmers destroying land for crops, tourists to Australia can also ruin bearded dragons' habitats if they are not careful.

their bearded dragons. In fact, it is illegal in most Australian states and territories to keep a dragon in captivity without a permit. And it is illegal to smuggle bearded dragons from Australia. These restrictions

It is important that humans take care of bearded dragons' habitats, so they can live in safe and healthy environments for many years to come.

have helped maintain bearded dragon populations in the past. And they will continue to help bearded dragons in the future.

Since the early 1960s, it has been illegal to take bearded dragons from Australia. This article in the online newspaper *PerthNow* explains how smuggling is still a problem in Australia:

> Two . . . men have been charged after attempting to smuggle 30 lizards out of Western Australia, worth up to $130,000 on the Asian black market.
>
> . . .
>
> State Environment Minister Albert Jacob, who is pushing for harsher penalties for wildlife smugglers, suggested the fines the men faced under the current Wildlife Conservation Act of up to $38,000 were not enough.
>
> "We need to ensure that wildlife smuggling attempts are met with the full force of the law," Mr. Jacob said.
>
> "They are not only illegal, but cruel and pose a risk to the state's unique and rich biodiversity."

Source: "Japanese Pair Charged over $130,000 Lizard Smuggling Attempt." PerthNow. News Ltd, October 3, 2013. Web. Accessed January 16, 2014.

Back It Up

The author of this passage is using evidence to support a point. Write a paragraph describing the point the author is making. Include two or three pieces of evidence the author uses to make the point.

Common Name: Bearded dragon

Scientific Name: *Pogona vitticeps*

Average Size: 4 to 24 inches (10 to 61 cm)

Average Weight: 10 to 18 ounces (283 to 510 g)

Color: Green, tan, yellow, and red

Average Life Span: Four to ten years in the wild; as pets, they may live longer

Diet: Small insects and lizards, rodents, leaves, and flowers

Habitat: Arid to semiarid areas, including deserts, dry forests, wooded areas, and dry grasslands

Predators: Eagles, hawks, bigger lizards, feral foxes, cats, snakes, and humans

Did You Know?

- Wild bearded dragons live alone and are able to take care of themselves from the time they hatch.
- Bearded dragons have unique gestures. They bob their heads and wave their front legs to communicate.
- Bearded dragons have venom glands but no fangs. They must bite hard on their small prey so the venom kills them.

Dig Deeper

After reading this book, what questions do you still have about bearded dragons? Write down one or two questions that can guide you in doing research. With an adult's help, find some reliable sources about bearded dragons that can help answer your questions. Write a few sentences about what you learned from your research.

You Are There

This book discusses how people who are camping or sightseeing sometimes destroy the habitats of bearded dragons. Imagine you own a tour company. You make your living by taking tourists into the Australian Outback. How can you take tourists to see the Outback without affecting the natural habitat? What list of rules would you give the tourists?

Take a Stand

This book discusses some of the problems that occur when bearded dragons and feral animals occupy the same areas. Do you think people should take greater steps to prevent bearded dragon habitat loss? Write a short essay explaining your opinion. Give facts and supporting details.

Tell the Tale

This book contains information about bearded dragons. Write a 200-word fictional story about bearded dragons. Use the knowledge you have gained from reading this book to describe the sights and sounds of these lizards that you witnessed.

GLOSSARY

adaptation
changing over multiple
generations to suit one's
environment

brumation
a kind of hibernation in which
body temperature falls and
appetite decreases

dingo
an Australian wild dog

endangered
a kind of animal that has
become rare and is in danger
of dying out completely

feral
an animal that has escaped
and become wild

omnivore
an animal that eats both
plants and animals

organ
a part of the body that
performs a specific function,
such as the heart or liver

semiarid
having light rainfall each year

submission
when one animal
acknowledges that another is
stronger or has more power

subtropical
regions and climates of the
world that border the tropics

LEARN MORE

Books

Mattison, Chris. *Bearded Dragons*. Hauppauge, NY: Barron's Educational Series, 2011.

Mazorlig, Tom. *Bearded Dragon*. Neptune City, NJ: TFH Publications, 2011.

Miller, Jake. *The Bearded Dragon*. New York: PowerKids, 2003.

Websites

To learn more about Amazing Reptiles, visit **booklinks.abdopublishing.com**. These links are routinely monitored and updated to provide the most current information available.

Visit **www.mycorelibrary.com** for free additional tools for teachers and students.

INDEX

ABOUT THE AUTHOR

Jody Jensen Shaffer is the author of 14 books for children and numerous poems and short fiction for magazines. She writes from the home she shares with her husband, two children, and dog in Missouri.

DATE DUE

PRINTED IN U.S.A.